Sonnet of a Housewife

and other poems

by Vickie Adair

3rd c

A Third Coast Publishers LLP Publication

Sonnet of a Housewife *and other poems*

First Edition

Text & Photographs Copyright © 2011
poetry by Vickie Adair • photography by Mikall Angela Hill

Cover design & book layout by Third Coast Publishers LLP.

All rights reserved. Printed in the United States of America.
No part of this book may be used or reproduced in any manner
whatsoever without written permission from the publishers.
Brief passages may be quoted for reviews.

Published by Third Coast Publishers LLP.

ISBN 978-0-9829498-2-5
Library of Congress Control Number: 2011922024

For more information and other publications visit:
www.ThirdCoastPublishers.com

In memory of Cyd Adams, my friend the poet.

~ Vickie ~

Table of Contents

SONNET OF A HOUSEWIFE 1
THE SQUAT-DOWN TREE 3
THE HORSE BREAKER 5
CHOCOLATE 6
CHECKING OUT AT WALGREENS 7
A CREEK IN THE WOODS 8
THE FALL 10
I, PUNISHED EVE 11
LEAVING LIGHT 13
THE COLD WAR 14
TO MELISSA, TIL NEXT TIME 16
DREAM JOURNEY 18
ABANDONED 20
BOAT TRIP INTO GULF 22
PLAIN WINDS 23
THE GARDENS OF HOTEL IXTAPAN 25
LOVER'S WORDS 27
THE DANCE 27
A QUARTER-OF-A-CENTURY AFTER THE BALL 28
SUNDAY AFTERNOON ENDING 29
A MOTHER'S SONG 31
SOMEDAY 33
THE TEACHER 35
THE BALLAD OF MAY LABEAUX 36
THE HOSPITAL 38
THE SILENCE 39
STEPS 40
MORNING RITUAL 41
WOMEN SHOULDN'T READ 42
WHAT THE DOC WANTS 44
THE LIFE BEAUTIFUL 46
SIXTIES SONG 48

CHILDREN GROWN	49
I'VE LOST TODAY	51
RAPUNZEL REFLECTS	52
PASSION'S STORM	55
BENEATH THE NEON STAR	56
NEAR SONNET TO ALMOST PARADISE, USVI	57
BESIDE A GRAVE	58
MY TREASURE CHEST	60
THE SWING	62
THANK YOU, KNEES	63
LOST FRIEND	65
MEMORIES LINGER	67
THE LAWS OF THINGS	68

Sonnet Of A Housewife

The heels of Donna Reed and Mrs. Cleaver's pearls

lit up the screens of black and white TV

back in fifty-eight. We were only girls

and TV told us how our lives should be.

I really tried my best till eighty-eight,

and even when the baby broke my beads,

I clung to TV's version of my fate,

and fixed my hair and met my family's needs.

Then cleaning out the shower wearing heels,

I slid across the soapy tiles, to slip

and grab the shower curtain just to reel

towards the floor to crash and cut my lip.

Reality defeats me—I concede!

I can't clean house and look like Donna Reed.

THE SQUAT-DOWN TREE

Most of my early days were spent loving a twisted tree,
my thin young arms and legs wrapped round rough bark.
Breathing in pine needle and rosin scents, I was free--
the tree trapped in deformity by lightning's fork.

One fork ran horizontal before reaching the sky;
the other stayed straight and true, towering above.
My daddy called it the Squat-Down Tree, and so did I,
but what I felt for that tree, I'm sure, was simply love.

Sitting in a branch, I first heard the universe's shout,
learned the sky has no end and neither does the now.
I sat in tune with the tree, no anxiety or doubt,
I learned such things later, we all do, one day, somehow.

Half a century's passed since I sat in the Squat-Down Tree,
But even now, when life gets hard, I go there in my mind.
Transport my soul to that tree and one more time feel free.
The world, not confined, gives what the soul finds.

THE HORSE BREAKER

Weekdays, he turned wrenches and adjusted bolts
---mundane, routine, repetitive chores---
beneath the blood-red Pegasus that soared
above confining rankness of refinery floors.

Evenings and weekends, he rode the horse
with black coat reflecting hues of blue, rebellious eyes
and nostrils flaring wide with rage, head held up
in defiant pride that should only come from freedom.

He rode every day but never tried to break the pride
of the kindred spirit also caged by a concrete world.
Then, never freed from refinery drudgery,
my father left silently to meet his death.

The fiercely noble horse was later put to sleep.
But sometimes under these unbroken Texas skies,
out on the edge where earth touches sunset,
I catch a glimpse of two freed spirits riding hard.

CHOCOLATE

One, two, I count to calm my nerves,
or better, eat a candy bar,
cause most times counting only serves
my agitation just so far.
Chocolate is where calm is at,
but what do I do with this fat?

Nervous counters seem to stay thin,
but I crave that chocolate taste.
Against my nerves it always wins,
but leaves some damage on my waist.
So should I count but always frown,
or smile and be a little round?

But better, I should find a way
to use thoughts as a healing balm,
think kind love and laugh everyday,
and thus maintain my inner calm.
Maybe if I accomplished that,
I could escape both frowns and fat!

Checking out at Walgreens

Looking past her grayed customer to me,

the young clerk said, "Sorry, for the wait."

Silently thankful to Nice & Easy

for my absence of gray, I hurried

to take money from my purse,

fearfully anticipating being looked past.

A certain slowing comes with time,

and the young have little patience.

The slowing comes- not so much from arthritis –

or weakness -but from a conscious knowing of now.

I no longer gulp morning coffee: I savor.

Being late doesn't seem like a disaster;

these days - it's the journey I enjoy.

It's true I do not move so swiftly now.

But some slowness is a choice to dawdle

through the day, loving each second alive.

A CREEK IN THE WOODS

Walking in a woods,

I come upon clear water,

rustling over rocks.

Rare shafts of sunlight

shine on the sparkling creek

in delightful play.

Moss covered branches

drape across the sacred scene,

my soul bounces back.

Near the mossy edge,

I sit beneath an old oak

and thank God for creeks.

THE FALL

After eons in paradise, the immortal Eve
Found existing dull and went to call on God.

Eve said to God, "I want to create and grow."
God answered, "The price is sweat and toil."

Eve said to God, "I want to laugh and love."
God answered, "The price is pain and grief."

Eve said to God, "I want to be alive."
God answered, "The price of life is death."

Eve said to God, "Just let me buy it all."
Smiling, God replied, "Here, just take a bite."

I, Punished Eve

Scream, sweat, strain

in childbirth,

lose sleep, answer cries,

clean diapers,

mop up filth.

I, the punished Eve,

hold my son's

captured frog,

watch my small daughter

playing mom,

dressing up.

I would not unbite

the apple.

I am Eve.

LEAVING LIGHT

Shivering

against a confederate gray sky,

brown leaves,

drained of their summer's green glory,

like you and I

were robbed of our red passions,

finally fall,

dying from the orbital flight

of an unaware world that could not slow its speed

so that leaves might revel in the light.

The Cold War

In the demilitarized zone
Of cloakrooms, boardrooms, desks,
Another promotion lost to the other sex.
He sweats with desire to walk,
Thinks of braces, electric bills,
And his recent engine overhaul,
Bites his lip, takes a breath.

But the homefront's under fire
Over economic policy
And territorial rights.
He listens to the soprano
Weapon drone on and on,
Wonders how Cinderella
Morphasized to MacArthur.

She looks at the kitchen table covered
With envelopes holding their bills,
Looks up to the eyes of her opponent
She'd promised to obey, respect
Under their original treaty.
But economic climates change,
She now earns the larger check.

He hears her tell their child
That she will talk to Dad,
And resents she has estranged him from
the one to be the victor's spoils.
While she resents that the child
Is too in awe of him to speak,
But sees in her no power, just a mom.

Neither of them can remember
When the gender wars began,
But know today amid the nuclear bombs,
Mastercards, and heavy metal bands,
It's grown from cold to battle hot.
He bites his lip and takes a breath.
She rubs her arms and sighs.

TO MELISSA, TIL NEXT TIME

My sister came for one of those two-day, extra-strength capsules

Of togetherness – good for our chronic isolation aches.

My son, crying, refused to join in farewell words, and I,

In artificial wisdom, said, good-bye just means "til next time."

My words connected in my slightly scrambled brain to you,

And how you refused Dylan's harsh advice

And wanted me to let you gently go.

Thoughts go full-circle, and I remembered recognizing you,

The first time we met, by the clarity in your eyes that

Looked straight to the truth of my Emmett Kelley soul.

I was glad to be seeing you again, and you me, but

I couldn't remember the life where we'd first met.

Probably next time I won't remember this time,

And probably you won't either, but you'll know me.

Among all the clowns you meet, I'll be unique.

And I'll know you, no matter what color some

Genetic roulette has made your eyes, they'll see clear.

DREAM JOURNEY

He walks ahead, over sun washed rocks.
Long, grey hair, held by leather band,
rises, falls against his straight, ancient back.
Behind, two small legs scurry in bent shadow.
In dream, the old one promised a great journey.

Near a river, on flat rock, rough and hot,
we sit, legs crossed on pink sandstone.
Raising weathered face, lined by nine decades,
he chants in an old tongue, teaching my spirit
to travel in the bodies of my brothers.

Crouching low, pink nose twitching,
sniffing familiar scents, dry dirt and grass,
I peer through the browning blades, whiskers quivering,
muscles tensing, anticipating my chance to spring
into the open sunshine toward the wetting of my tongue.

Darting through cool water, swaying plants,
feeling scales bend as my body flexes,
the pulsing flow of water through my gills,
I stretch hard lips wide, win a wriggling mouthful,
sink to sandy bed through dancing green.

Lowering moist nose to ground, sensing danger,
I ease forward, skin drawing tight, bunching at neck,
hairs standing, lips curling back, throat rumbling.
Muscles tense for every controlled step that warms
my pads with hot dirt. Restraining power, I am.

The old one calls. Encloses my small hand
in his dry, wrinkled palm, then rises.
Legs, dimpled by gritty rock, turn toward waking.
He walks beside, over shadowed rocks,
long, grey hair lifting in evening wind.

ABANDONED

Do not walk so close behind, Old Wolf.

I am too old to walk with you;

Too many years have been spent

Envying the blue and green eyes of my sisters.

Do not howl beneath my moon, Old Wolf.

I am too busy with corporate cocktail parties,

Green money and silver screened realities

To walk with you right now.

Do not call my true name, Old Wolf.

I am someone else these days,

Listening to the call of market funds and power.

I am afraid to heed your call, Old Wolf.

Old Wolf?

Boat Trip Into Gulf

Pushing off from pier,
The boat, rubbing shack-lined shore,
brings canal in view.

Passing traffic pounds
Beat of barges, tugboats throb.
Shrimp boats throttle down.

Sunlight touching tops
Of ripping waves, sparks tiny
orbs of dancing light.

Heading out to deep,
Trailed by boiling wake of white,
The boat gathers speed.

Hours out from shore,
the boat, anchor thrown in waves,
takes a well-earned rest.

Backs on shrimp boat near
Heave and breathe and heave again
in dance with their nets.

Seagulls shriek across
The sky, swooping down to fish
In rolling blue-green crest.

Dark and glistening wet,
In rolling, rhythmic motion,
Backs of dolphins curve.

Glowing amber sun,
Falls toward the horizon,
Tints the liquid hills.

Coastward turns the boat,
The white whirling wake reversed,
Leaving water churned.

On the freeway home,
Inner ear still hears the gulls,
and waves lapping hull

PLAIN WINDS

Summer's heaving puffs
touch dry dirt where maize once grew,
bending with the breeze.

Gusts uncover flint
that flew and failed the hunt,
found its grave instead.

Through adobe ruins,
the wind, gasping through the rooms,
sounds a lonely wail.

Brushing broken bowls,
Earth's breath of life caresses
memories of maize.

THE GARDENS OF HOTEL IXTAPAN

My sisters left with a group of brisk morning walkers,

and I made a solitary turn toward the gardens briefly glimpsed.

The expanse of dark tropical foliage and old canopied trees

sprinkled with vined flowers suddenly in view

stunned my eyes with still beauty glistened with dew.

Rare silence drowned the normal clatter of my brain.

Meandering down the garden path, I smelled the soothing

scents that only life, and earth, and water can produce.

In a far corner, an ancient oak filled me with desire, like lust,

to embrace its giant grayed limbs and find a refuge there.

Then my sisters' voices echoing down the path called to me;

I left the tree, to walk toward the shelter of my sisters' love.

LOVER'S WORDS

If only I could write a symphony
of words that sang with laughs and rage,
my pen could let my thoughts fly free
with words that run and fall across the page.

In black and white, I'd tell my deepest pain,
write the winds across the arid lands.
describe the way I smell a summer rain,
and put my tears into your loving hands.

Though often to each other's arms we go,
Without the words, it's me you'll never know.

THE DANCE

To the rhythm of Elvis, you and I
spun in synchronized steps across the floor,
eyes as entwined as our slender young arms.

Now, we jerk to some heavy-metal scream,
moving alone on the electric floor,
never seeing, never touching, the other.

A Quarter-of-a-Century After The Ball

He calls me Cinder still,

only the tone has changed,

and now it is a fitting name

to represent all charred remains

of a distant ballroom flame.

Since then I have obtained

broadened hips and breast that swing

giving Princelings to the King,

but Charming is charming still

to ladies-maids, kitchen girls,

that young duchess with golden curls.

"Cinder," his royal voice barks,

and I go, a cinder gray and chill,

except for the flicker of a spark

that tells me take that glass spiked-heel

and throw it like a dart.

SUNDAY AFTERNOON ENDING

The ice of your eyes,

rejecting my help,

blows an Arctic wind,

swirls my long collection

of recollections…..chest pains

from rumors of Monterrey whores,

cuts from ridiculed competence,

nausea from the woman's call….

Then the swift swing of your hand,

meant to wave me out of your way,

blows old wounds to painless.

A MOTHER'S SONG

I drive life's super sonic freeway
Made of concrete, steel, and rails.
Clutching offspring in shells of fragile flesh,
I gather speed to a frantic pace.
    I honk
               and skid
                           and race
. . . no choice of destination.
There are no exits in the rail.
Desperation grows as miles of pavement
Zoom beneath my feet.
Speeding through the night alone—afraid,
I dream of crashing through the rail
to find my fragile ones a trail of dirt
that meanders across the earth.
                            ---Horns honk!
                Dreams fade.
There are no breaks ….
   . . . but, if I had the power of God,
I'd knock this freeway down ---
and build a Garden here.

SOMEDAY

A loaded sink with dirty dishes waits,
And my student's graded papers are late.
The household bills are in a mess,
And, God! I hate the IRS!

One kid has got to get to Boy Scouts;
one just wants to get with friends to go out.
The spouse is out - with all my cash,
And I am left to carry out the trash.

I cannot love you in insanity
of duty, ethics, and reality.
I dream someday we join as one,
somewhere not beneath earth's sun.

The Teacher

They told me they could make my son

a perfect little English pea,

smooth out his edges every one,

change brown to green as it should be,

until the differences were none

between him and every other pea.

I told them I just didn't think

He really wanted to be green.

They said I should see a shrink—

I sounded like a pinto bean.

So I shut up and tried to look around,

hoping they didn't see I was brown.

The Ballad of MAY LaBEAUX

In the south of Louisiana,
The swamps way down low,
There lives the craziest woman.
Her name is May LaBeaux.

They say she had a brown-eyed son,
Gift of a roaming rake.
The child was her consuming love,
Her brown-eyed boy called Jake.

One frozen day of Jake's fifth year,
To May LaBeaux's front door,
Came the people of her town,
Her dead son Jake they bore.

Her scream sent shudders through the crowd;
It echoes still today.
No longer did May hear the world;
Her mind had gone away.

The small swamp town she walks alone
Inward always listening,
As if she hears some sad refrain,
Her eyes always glistening.

She stops a stranger now and then,
And asks as if a'dreaming,
"Oh, do you hear my babe's soft laugh,
Or hear my soul a'screaming?"

THE HOSPITAL

Carts rush.

Feet race.

Steel gleams.

Lights blind.

Someone drops a metal tray.

Gloves grab.

Smells gag.

Palms push.

Dials plunge.

Someone shouts down the hall.

IV drips.

Sheets drape.

Sights freeze.

Sounds still.

Someone whispers you are dead.

THE SILENCE

I pray, begging incoherently,
while my son draws shuddering breaths
until the room dissolves.

Here from Hell's abyss,
Somewhere past pain,
I embrace the sanity of rage.
Toss down the gauntlet Satan threw.

But gauntlet, like my begging,
is met with silence.

STEPS

Walking, feet naked, in moist plowed dirt,
behind my dad's bare, sweating back draped
with leather reins, I stretch legs, trying
to reach his tracks, fail with every step.
I breathe the scent of freshly upturned earth,
hear sounds of birds and crickets crying.

Feet in sharp shoes tapping city streets,
walking the steel material world,
I reach out for MasterCards and cars,
better schools for kids, a bigger house.
I breathe the scent of cigarette fumes,
hear sounds of ice clinking glass in bars.

Feet frozen in Nieman-Marcus shoes,
I stand just inside the milk-white room
while my son shudders in deathly dreams,
gasps for breath, then stills beyond my reach.
I breathe the scent of cold funeral flowers,
hear the sound of endless silent screams.

Walking, feet booted, through yester-doors,
I search for absolution in words,
follow the Ox backward down the trail,
free the child walking bare-foot in the dirt.
I breathe the scent of freshly upturned earth,
hear screams' echoe fade into the smell.

MORNING RITUAL

Slicing silence, his calling voice
opens my eyes to the pre-dawn gray.
The voice fading in the still shadows
chills my lungs to cold, hard steel—

weight—carried by my chest
in search of salvation's black brew
to burn my tightened throat
trained in holding back the flood.

After caffeine and nicotine
steady hands smear stage-thick greasepaint
to the semblance of a smile.
Charcoal liner completes the mask—

hiding truth—so I find
strength to lunge toward the door.
Feet stumble, anticipating
dawn's next gray and his calling voice,

when blade-sharp morning knowledge
that my son will not rise to lighten gray
sends me rushing for the shelter
found only in numbing work-day rituals.

WOMEN SHOULDN'T READ

I had an English teacher
Who touched on what we women need,
asking, "What would you be if you
Had never learned to read?"

I was stunned at the word
That quickly popped into my head.
If I screamed out, "Happy! Happy!"
Would my teacher fall down dead?

I might have lived in ignorant bliss
A domesticated life.
I might have learned by now
To be a proper wife.

And might have to my little children
Been a soothing sun's ray,
Believed everything the preacher said,
Not known the world was gray.

But instead I read of many things,
Like gods, men, and apple pie
And found ten million whys – or one –
Like why do children die?

The prose I read made me want
To scream – or maybe kill.
The books I read to find an answer
Brought more questions still.

I turned then to the poets
The answers they must surely know,
But Emily deceived me, and
My leg was pulled by Poe.

What the Doc Wants

The Doctor says I'm Crazy
So he gives me little pills.
They make my thoughts all hazy
And my stomach deathly ill

With my head above the toilet,
I wonder---------
    " God, am I happy, yet?"

Terrors walk my dreams at night
So Doc prescribes some Retoril,
Little capsules red and white,
My mighty dreams to steal.

Then asks of dreams that never came
To determine----------
    If I'm now sane!

A boy in therapy with me
Drew a house for the Docs,
But forgot to add a chimney,
Showing lack of warmth that shocks.

Since the kid never saw a fireplace,
I think----------
"There's connection in this case?"

Our problem is that we are round.
Doc's squaring us to fit the cubicle
Where he says we should be found,
And deems any treatment usable.

We're trying to conform with little fuss,
But I wonder----------
    "Then, will we still be us?"

the life beautiful

The deepest bliss I ever feel
comes when I am quiet and still.
A symphony of silence softly touches
every fiber of my seeking mind.

Like the oak tree, living in the now,
simply grows, silently, serene, and great,
I grow stronger being in the calm
to obliterate my storms of grief.

Afterwards, laughter starts to stir,
like sunshine prickling on my skin.
Sounds of nature's glee fall in my ear,
and beauty drapes my pretty days.

Sixties Song

We flaunted youth's arrogant strength,

Overpowered our parents and past,

Stoned holocaust stories with silence,

And waged our war in American streets,

Waving signs that threatened peace.

Our gods came in powder and smoke,

Our Angels wore leather and chains.

Children Grown

Now our children come to youthful power,

and they less arrogant, or perhaps nobler, than we

accept aging angels with amused tolerance,

allow our old rock idols to remain on stage,

often ask about the past, the one we can't explain,

of signs and songs and wars waged in the streets

in the name of love and peace.

I'VE LOST TODAY

Living out here in the land of tomorrow

writing the great American story,

growing skinny with some magic,

and making more money than old Midas,

I've lost my way back to my today.

Living trapped somewhere in yesterday

letting mommy clean house,

taking money from a Daddy Tree,

and having young men lust for the firmer me,

I can't remember how to find my now.

RAPUNZEL REFLECTS

She warned me that men would come,
Forbade me to let down my hair.
Then the prince came to my tower,
So tall and sweet and, oh, so fair.

Of course, he wanted exactly
What the witch had said he would,
Begged, then satisfied himself.
For me, it wasn't even good.

After, he said he feared the witch
And wanted me to get him out,
No thought for how I feared the witch,
Or what his weight did to my scalp.

When the witch saw I was with child,
She drove me from my tower home.
I found no shelter, for my shame,
And shunned, I bore my twins alone.

For one seven minute sin,
I'd paid for seven long, hard years
Before I found that prince at last
And cured his curse with salty tears.

I thought my punishment was over.
But, for thirty years—every day—
I've listened to him curse me for
The price he says he had to pay.

Passion's Storm

When it comes, like a lightening storm of lust,

my reasoning mind wages war with passion,

but desire resurrects unattended

from the hot steamy ashes of its death.

Passion's power, flesh daring wild delights,

a pleading sigh, overcomes all reason

or threats of a forbidden scarlet stain.

Wild waves of pleasure can not be repressed.

If other tongues rage scorn and whisper shame,

then guilt must bind us, and lust take the blame.

Beneath The Neon Star

Tonight, the Nacalina Lounge,
a local lakeside bar,
calls to my car to come and park
beneath its neon star.

In smoky light, I sit beside
a graying, broken man,
who worked in oilfields forty years,
faced death's waiting hand.

We talk about the weather some,
then talk some useless jive.
and when the drink has freed our tongues,
we talk about our lives.

I talk about my pile of bills,
of wanting to break free and run.
While Willie makes the jukebox wail,
the man speaks of things not done.

Near Sonnet to Almost Paradise, USVI

Crack-man, crazy-man, in exhaust streams,
Your dreadlocks swing with a no-rhythm beat.
Dancing the tunes of your crack induced dreams,
you flail and fling your odorous feet.

Away from all our digested clover,
cracky and crazy, you still feel the mess,
for your seam-rotted shirt just moved over
for a perfumed blond in a Dior dress.

Born to the sound of crystalline seas,
Raised on papaya and Eden-mango,
living your life in the warm salty breeze,
Oh, crack-man, crazy-man, didn't you know:

The Garden-deception of this tropic isle
is no protection from a serpent's smile.

BESIDE A GRAVE

Scents of old Spice and sweat-soaked shirts
are lost against the tangy smell of dirt.

Songs of love and many lusty tunes
go still below the silent grassy dune.

Sounds of frequent guffawed roars
freeze in shade of sheltering oak.

Legs that always walked against the tide
Conform beneath green rolling rows.

Late afternoon, the name in stone
Casts a shadow upon rolling ground.

MY TREASURE CHEST

A simple soul, I'm easily showered with wealth—

The smell of fresh cut grass and salty seas,

Those unforgotten nights of love and stealth,

Remembered jumps on piles of autumn leaves,

That old twisted pine I loved and still recall,

A sleeping child that snuggled near my breast,

Sometimes I even love the sparkles of the mall!

Please, Death, don't take this treasure chest.

THE SWING

Digging toes in the dirt, I shove off for the air.
Like Pegasus, the child-sized strip of wood,
Harnessed to fly only repetitive arcs,
Jerks the iron chains and rears at Olympus.
Spurring air, the rider escapes confining arcs.

Bowing her body and slicing the wind,
Annie digs heels in the stallion's black sides,
Leans forward and flees from Billy the Kid.

Squinting at leaves spinning back from her face,
Lee steers her spaceship away from the sun,
Speeds for the stars of Alpha Centauri.

Watching the ground rise on the down glide,
She-ra rides the vine to jungle's green heart,
Fights to free Cheeta from a hunter's snare.

From a near-by window, my mother's voice calls
And pulls me back from my arc-lived lives.

Thank You, Knees

My right knee hurts this afternoon,
from years of over use.
Such aching pains don't come too soon;
we were made for abuse.

I jumped from my roof at three,
twisted my knee at five,
fell off a mule, and from a tree.
It's a wonder I'm alive.

In my twenties, I was a klutz,
stumbled around in heels.
damaged my knees with frequent cuts,
and four more decades reeled.

Now when my knee starts hurting me,
I remember those days
of stumbling and jumping free.
Thank you, knees, for the memories!

LOST FRIEND

Her brown-eyed daughter lies asleep at last

And now there's dirty laundry still to face.

While sadness from an old tape player blasts,

She picks up toys, finding each its place,

Then shutters at her frightening stack of debt

And reaches for a glass to pour a shot.

She takes a gulp and lights a cigarette,

Regrets the teacher conference she forgot,

And looks toward the million nights to come,

Turns on TV so she won't be alone.

She takes another gulp or two of rum

And sits beside her enemy the phone.

Then later, with a lover-like caress,

She pulls the shotgun near her breast.

Memories Linger

Memories linger tucked away,
silent four decades, maybe more,
until jogged into the now today
by just your moving through the door.

Some little movement of your feet,
I recognized from our last brush.
A memory unfurls complete:
scent, sound, but mainly touch.
 The night air blows across our bed
through the open window of spring.
Scents of day lilies fill my head,
your soap scent captures me and clings.

Your warm body lays next to mine,
warm as only young skin can be.
It was just once upon a time,
But it made me remember me.

The Laws of Things

The underlying laws of things perpetually shift by degrees,

but bizarre possibilities seem latent in these changing seas.

Newton's law of gravity ruled for half a millennium it seems;

now falling from the sky is not sure, a law of lift supersedes.

So, can't there be some reckless quantum law of the wind

that allows every artificial wish I could imagine to blow in.

First, I'd be agreeable to wealth, then health and being thin.

I'd stray away from this world - to some world I'd comprehend.

Perhaps in reality, my desires can't be met by having much,

but I believe the law exists that lets me soar by being much.

About the Author

For the past thirty-one years, Vickie Adair has taught writing at the university, college, and corporate levels and worked as a freelance writer. Her first book publication was an illustrated children's book entitled *Once Upon a Tooth...a fairy's tale*. Over the years, she wrote poems for herself more as a means of therapy than for publication, but has recently been persuaded to release them to her publisher. With the exception of a few poems that were printed in a university magazine, this collection marks the first publication of her poetry.

Vickie currently resides in Houston, Texas.

Read her Storyteller's Blog:

www.vickieadair.com

Follow her on Twitter:

www.twitter.com/Vickie_Adair

Friend her on Facebook:

Search for "Vickie Adair"

Buy her Children's Book on Amazon:

Search for "Once Upon a Tooth... a Fairy's Tale"
Available in hardcover or for download on the Kindle

OTHER REVIEWS

A collection of reflective, thought-provoking poems, dealing with subjects including age, death, tragedy, relationships, truth, and loneliness. Some are poignant and moving, others are humourous, but all are tied together by the common thread of undeniable wisdom shining out from the written words. An anthology of verse in which the author uses nostalgia and memories to deliver her message that more often than not it is the simple things in life that mean the most.

Maria Savva, author of 'A Time to Tell' and 'Second Chances'

"Vickie Adair's poetry is smart, because it makes you smile and tear up and shake your head in both recognition and disbelief. It's smart ass because she is able to do this and make it rhyme occasionally too. I hate bad poetry. Vickie writes the kind I love."

Tim Bryant, author of Dutch Curridge

ACKNOWLEDGEMENTS

Thank you to our gracious reviewers. We appreciate the time you gave reading the book and supplying feedback.

Visit **Harry Leslie Smith**'s site to purchase his book: www.1923thebook.ca

Find **Valerie Sweeten** on Facebook; she always posts links to her stories online!

Learn more about **Maria Savva** at: www.mariasavva.com. or www.twitter.com/Maria_Savva

Visit **Tim Bryant**'s site to learn more about him and his works: www.bytimbryant.weebly.com

www.ingramcontent.com/pod-product-compliance
Lightning Source LLC
LaVergne TN
LVHW052256070426
835507LV00035B/3044